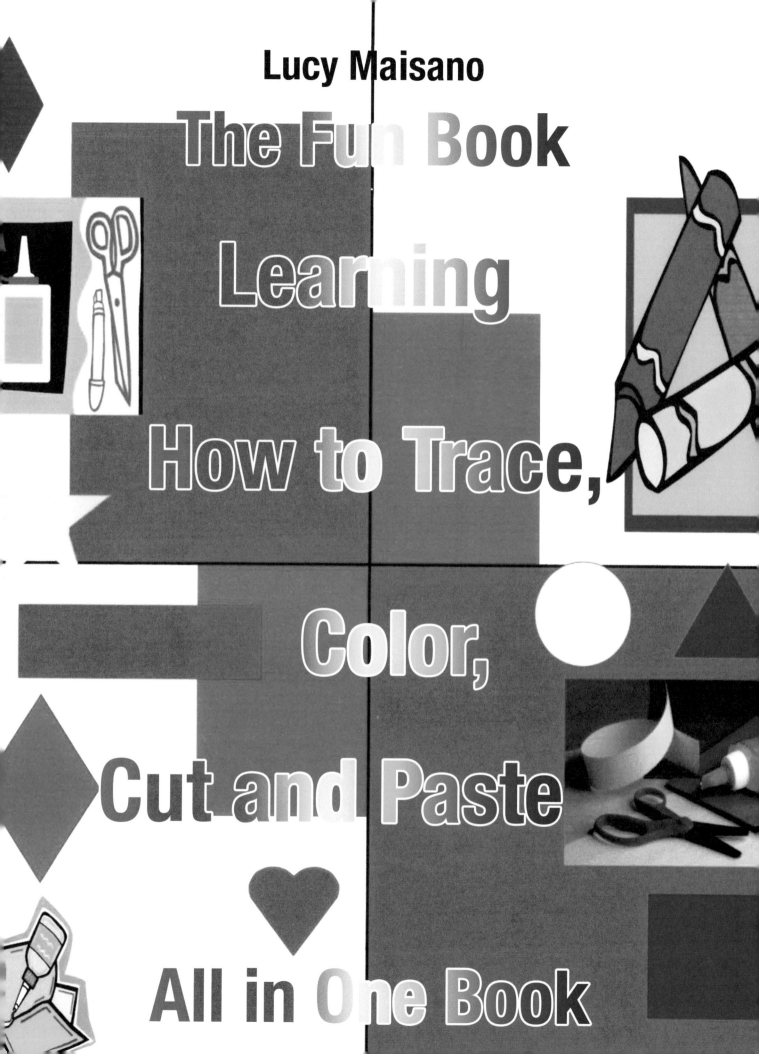

Lucy Maisano

# The Fun Book

## Learning

## How to Trace,

## Color,

## Cut and Paste

## All in One Book

AuthorHouse™
1663 Liberty Drive
Bloomington, IN 47403
www.authorhouse.com
Phone: 833-262-8899

This book is printed on acid-free paper.

ISBN: 978-1-6655-2069-0 (sc)
ISBN: 978-1-6655-2070-6 (e)

Print information available on the last page.

Published by AuthorHouse  05/21/2021

authorHOUSE®

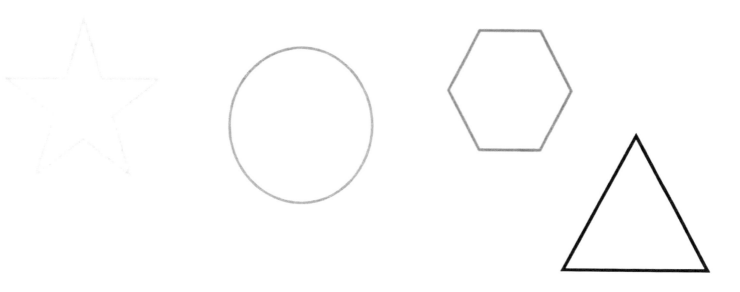

THE FUN BOOK OFFERS FUN PAGES

1. YOU WILL FIND TRACE AND COLOR THIS WILL HELP YOUR CHILD TO STAY IN THE LINES
2. YOU WILL ALSO FIND THE BONUS PAGES MATCH THE SHAPES AND COLORS
3. YOU WILL FIND COLOR IN THE SHAPES THIS WILL HELP YOUR CHILD TO IDENTIFY THE SHAPES
4. AFTER YOUR CHILD HAS LEARNED HOW TO TRACE COLOR AND MATCH UP SHAPES THEY WILL LOVE TO LEARN HOW TO COLOR CUT AND PASTE IN THE FUN BOOK

HAVE FUN LEARNING IN THE FUN BOOK!

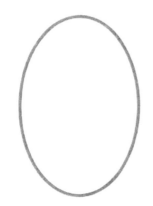

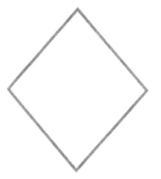

Who thought learning could be so much fun

Trace and color

Match the shapes and color (Bonus pages)

Color in the shapes

After practicing:

Tracing and coloring

Matching up shapes

Color the shapes that match

You will find color cut and past

It's so much fun

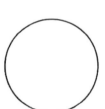

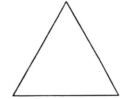

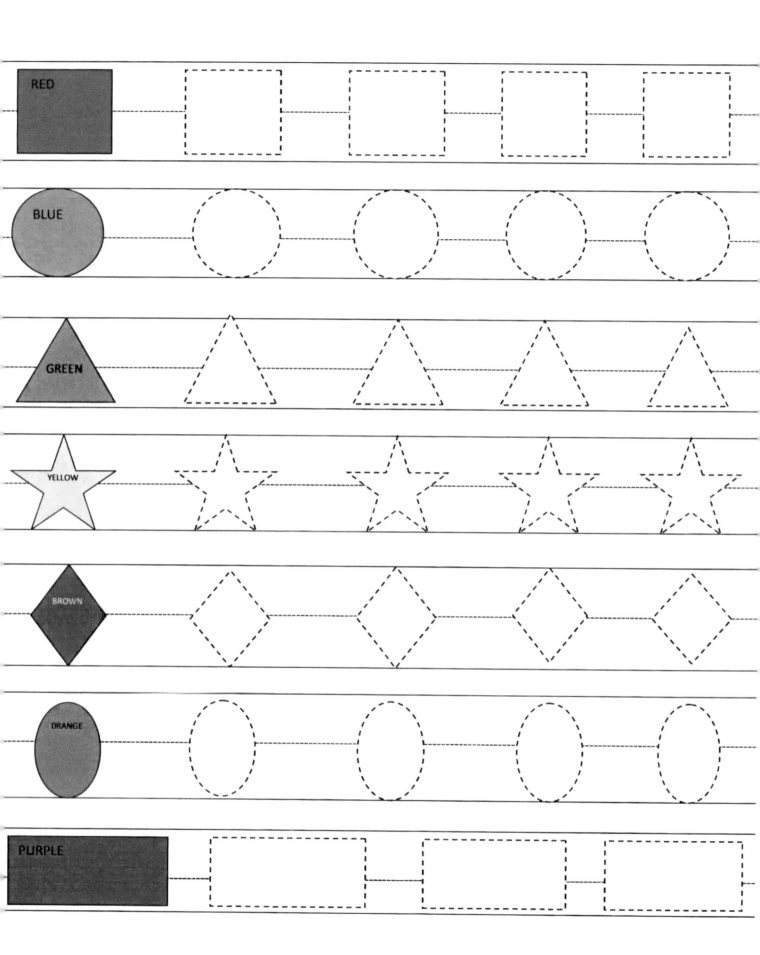

Learn your colors and shapes with THE FUN BOOK

# Trace and color shape

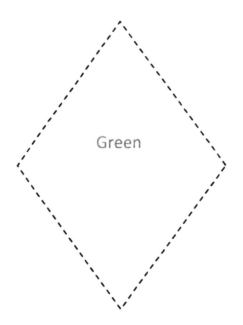

Green

Blue

# Trace and color shape

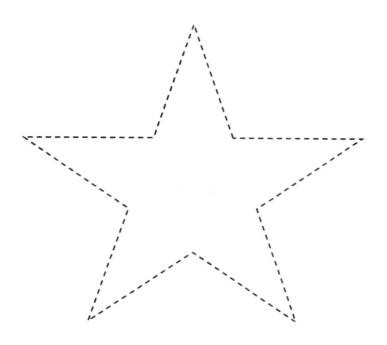

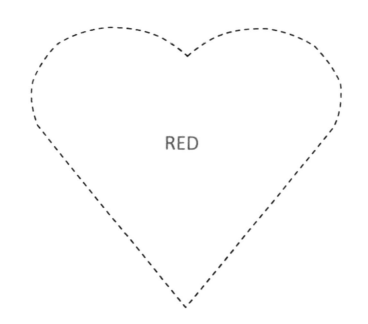

RED

TRACE AND COLOR IN YOUR FAVORITE COLORS

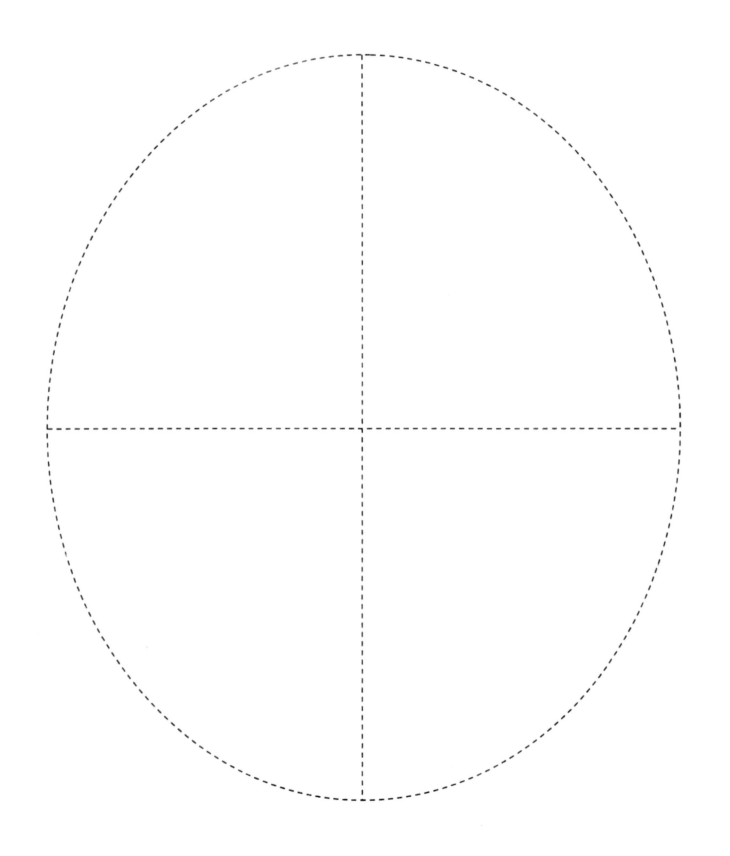

# Trace and color shapes

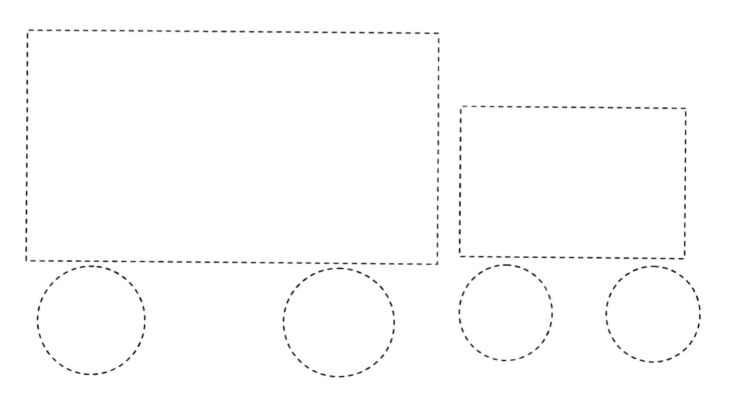

# TRACE AND COLOR IN THE BALLOONS AND BIRTHDAY HAT

COLOR THE WATER BLUE AND TRACE THE
STARS AND COLOR YELLOW

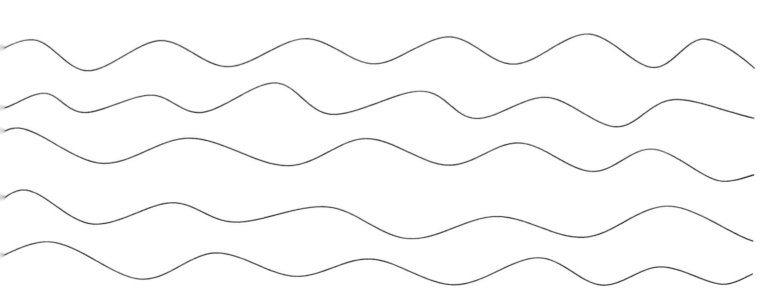

Trace and color in the shapes with your favorite colors

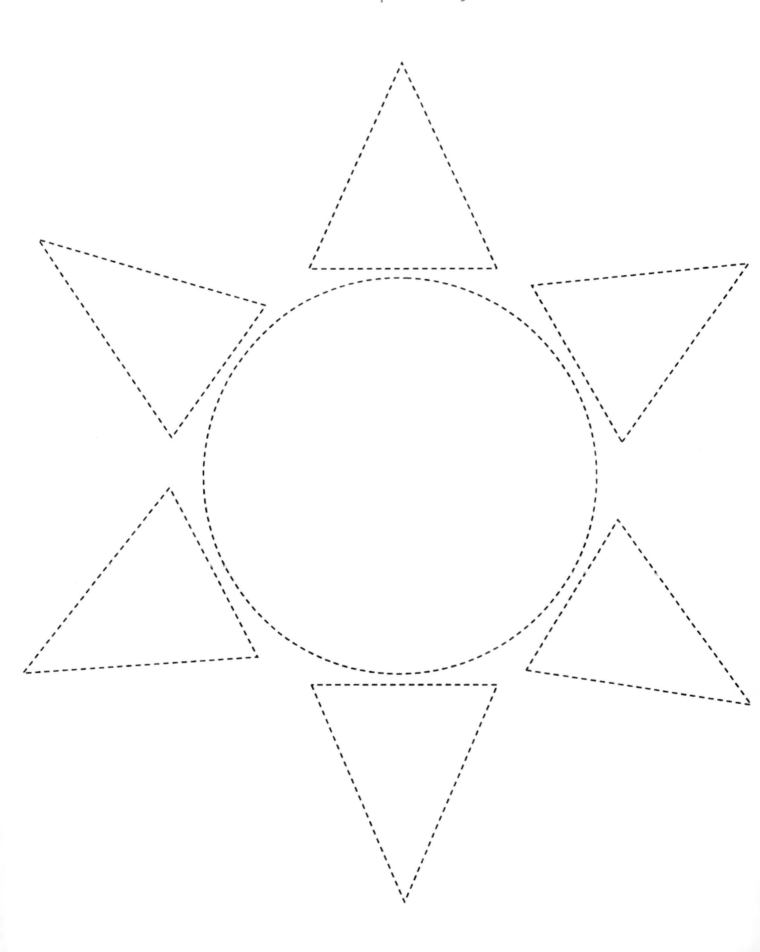

# TRACE AND COLOR IN YOUR THREE FAVORITE CRAYON COLORS

## HAVE FUN SHOWING YOUR FAVORITE COLORS

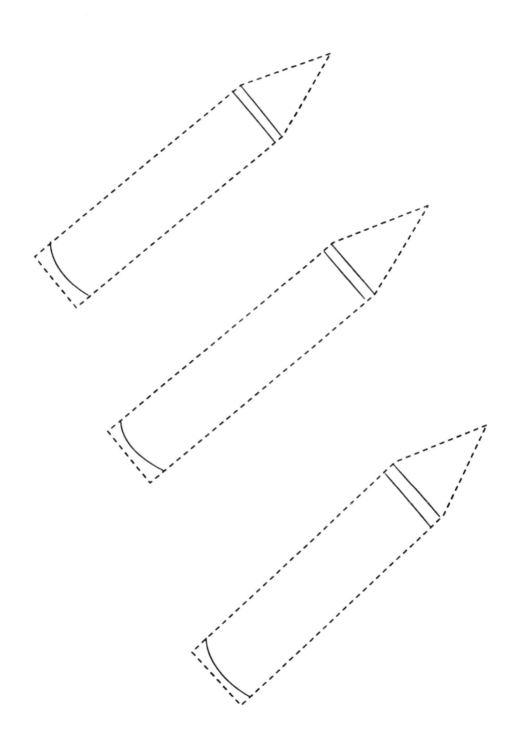

# THE FUN BOOK

## BONUS
## PAGES

## MATCH UP
## SHAPES
## AND
## COLORS

# COLOR IN THE SHAPE THAT MATCH

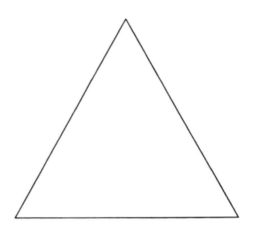

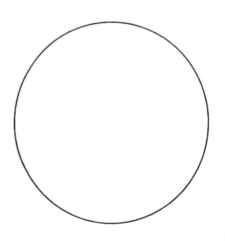

# COLOR THE SHAPE TO MATCH

# COLOR THE SHAPE TO MATCH

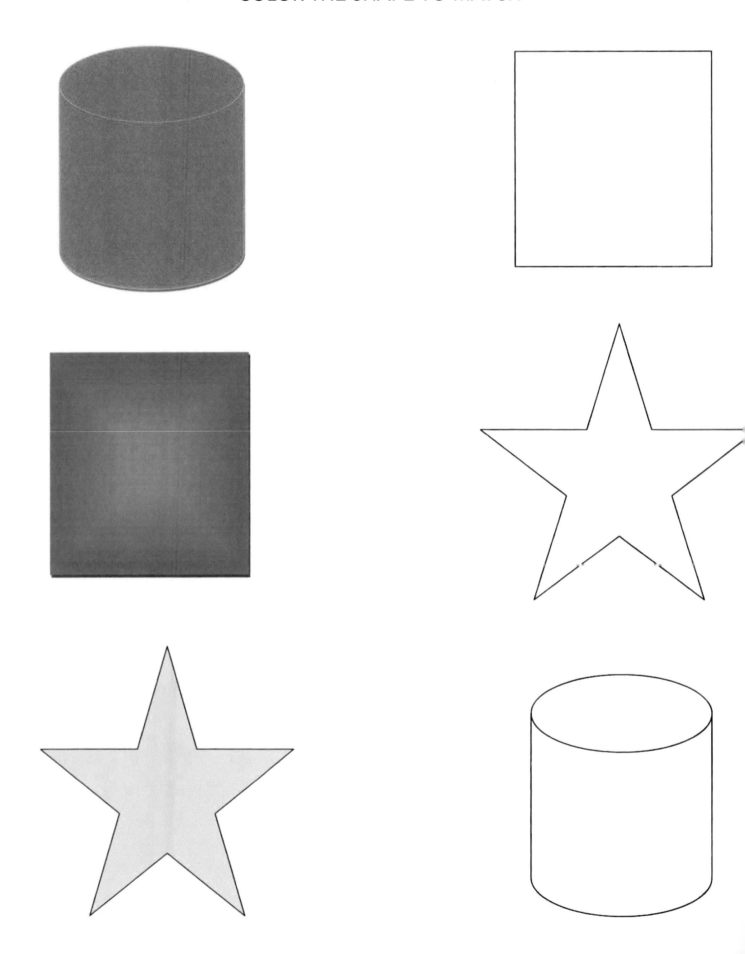

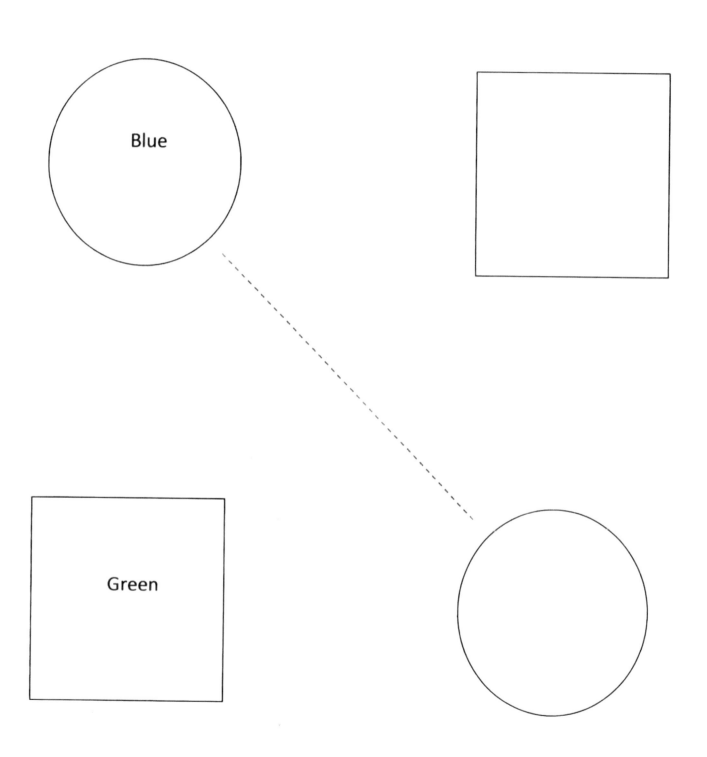

# Color to match

## Make up your own matching colors

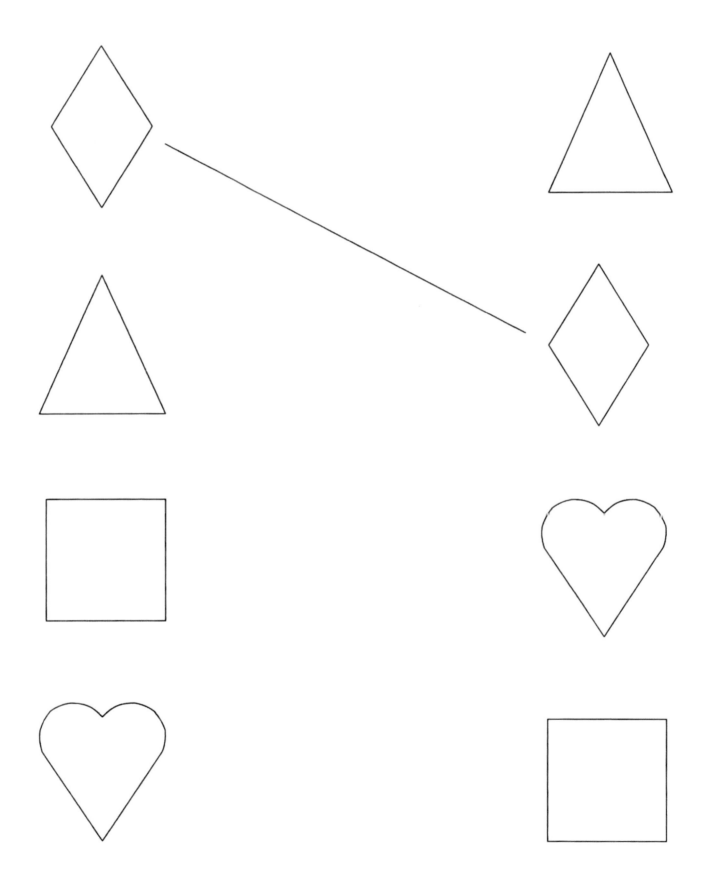

# THE FUN BOOK

## COLOR
## IN THE
## SHAPES

# Color the same shape to match

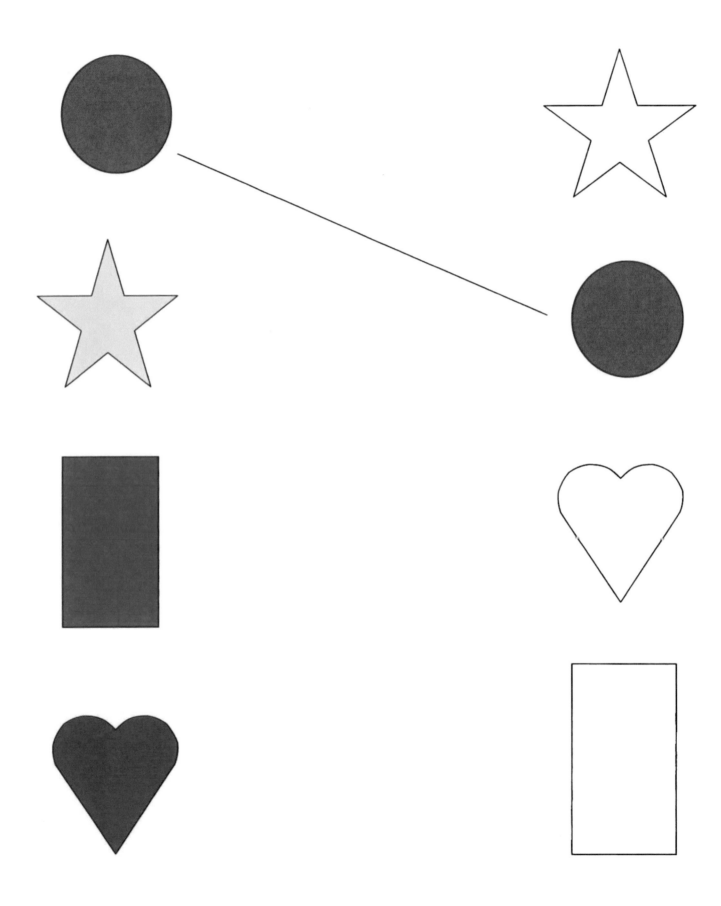

COLOR THE CIRCLE RED COLOR THE TRIANGLE COLOR
THE OVAL GREEN COLOR THE SQUARE PURPLE

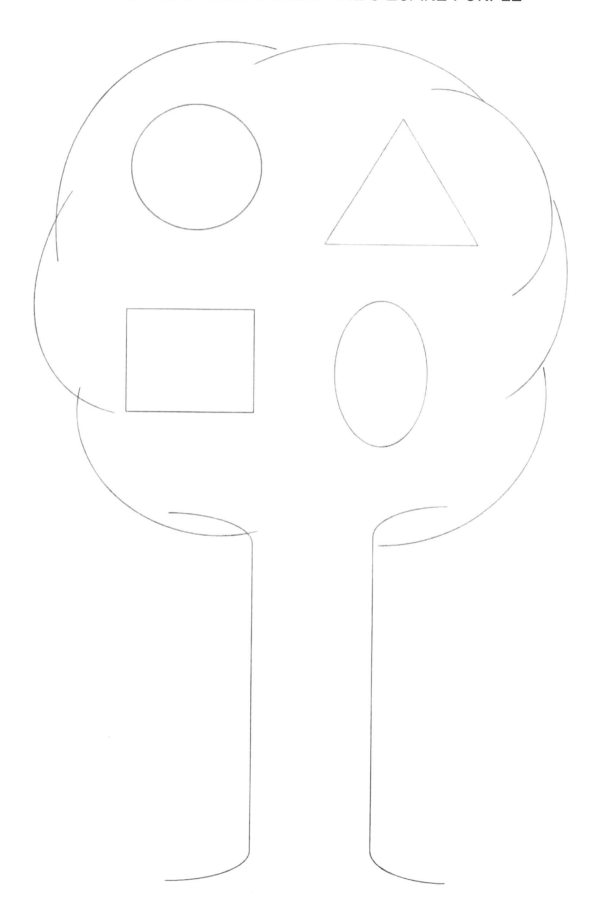

# COLOR IN THE BEACH BALL

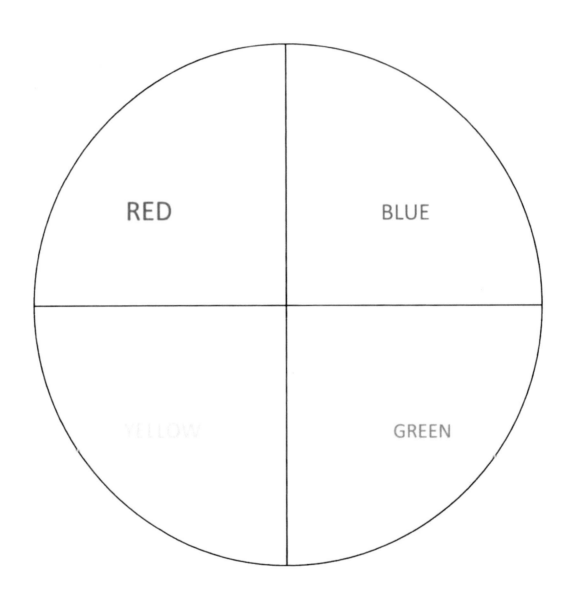

# COLOR THE SHAPES IN THE SKY

# Color in the cherries on the Tree

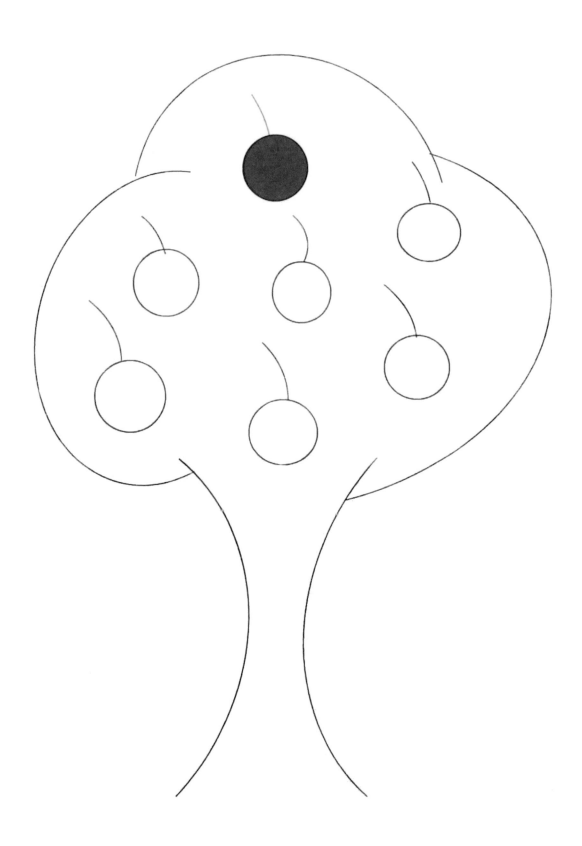

# THE FUN BOOK

# WILL TEACH
# YOUR CHILD
# HOW TO
# COLOR, CUT AND
# PASTE

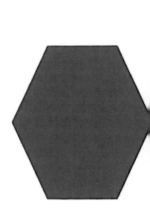

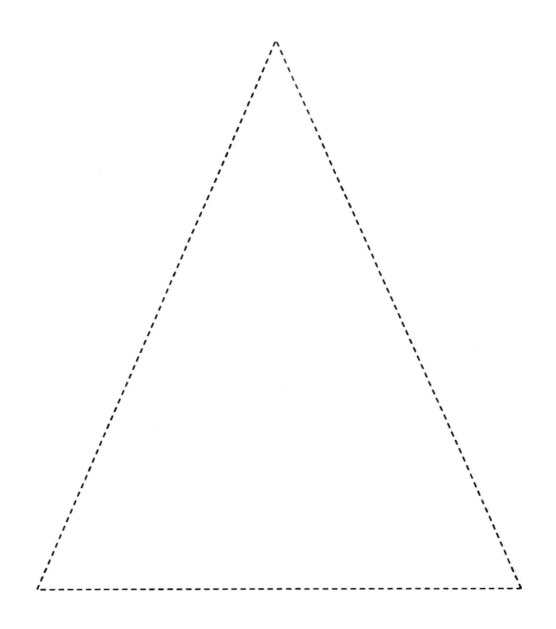

# TRIANGLE

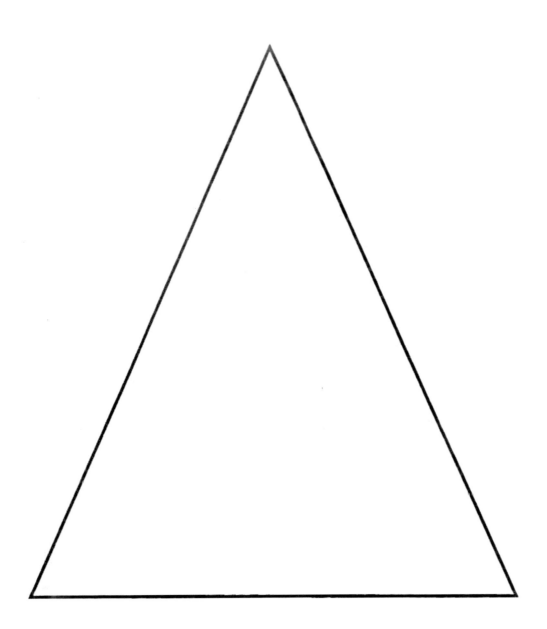

# SQUARE SHAPE

# CIRCLE SHAPE

TRACE COLOR AND CUT AND PASTE TO NEXT PAGE

# RECTANGLE SHAPE

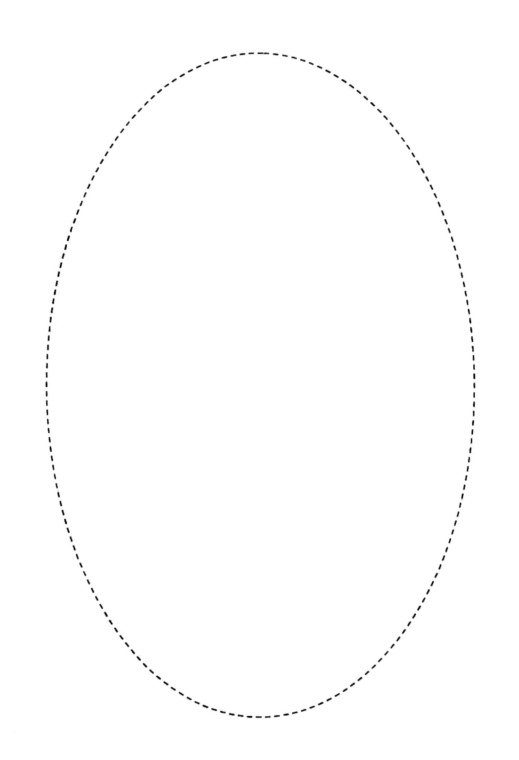

OVAL SHAPE

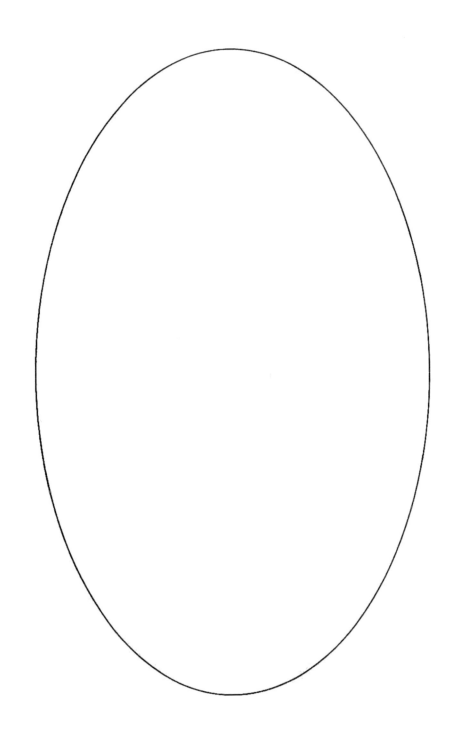

TRACE COLOR AND CUT AND PASTE TO NEXT PAGE

# STAR SHAPE

TRACE COLOR AND CUT AND PASTE TO NEXT PAGE

# TREE AND HOUSE MADE OUT OF SHAPES

TRACE COLOR AND CUT AND PASTE TO NEXT PAGE

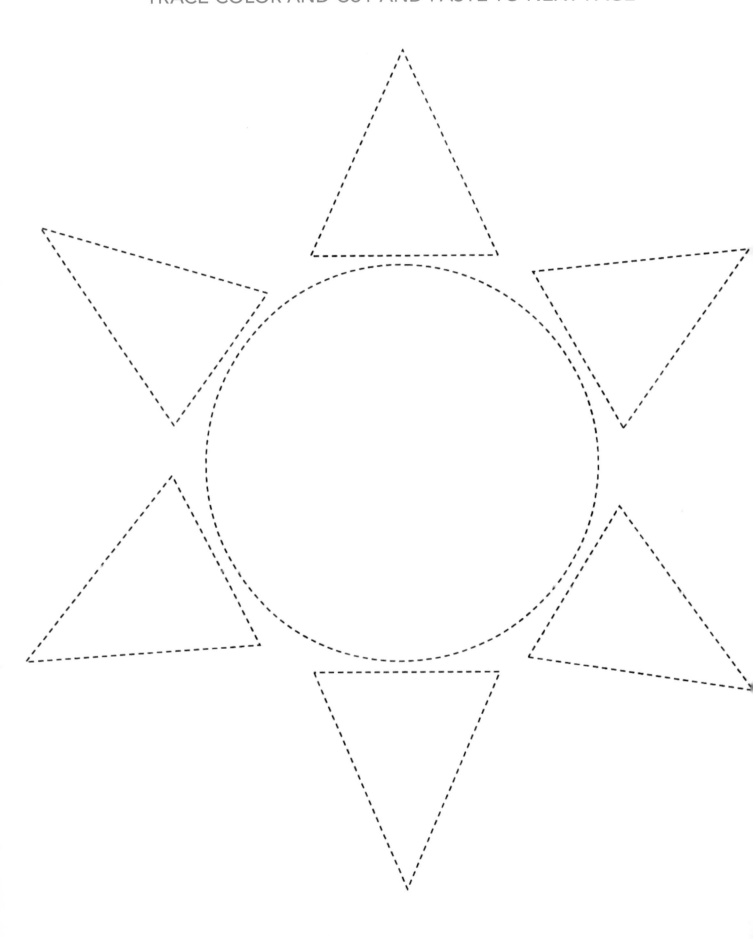

SUN

# HOUSE AND MOON

TRACE COLOR AND CUT AND PASTE TO NEXT PAGE

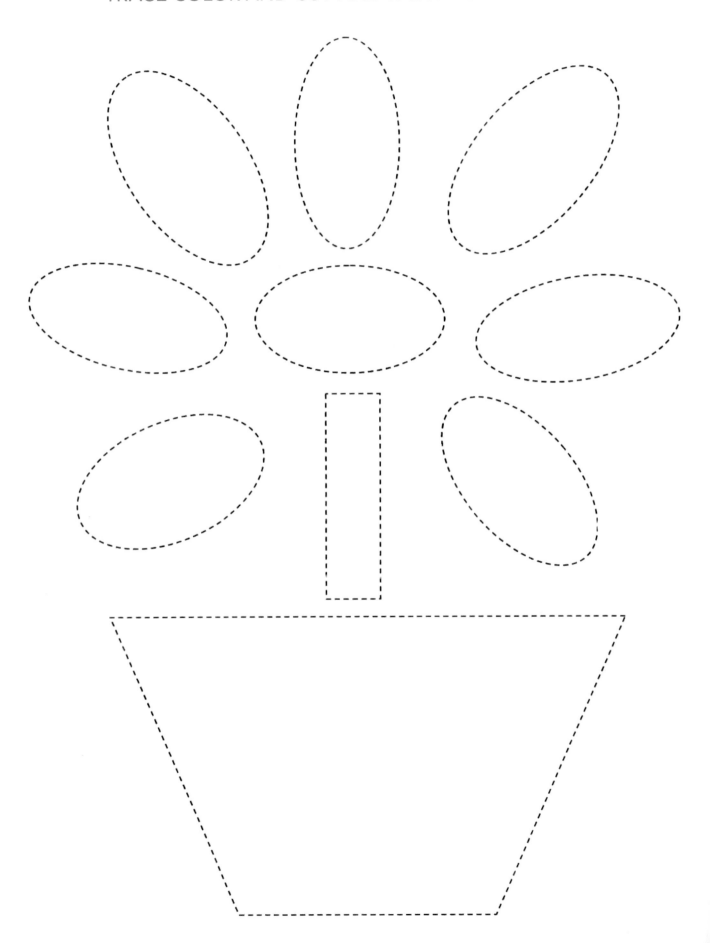

FLOWER

Trace color and cut and paste to next page

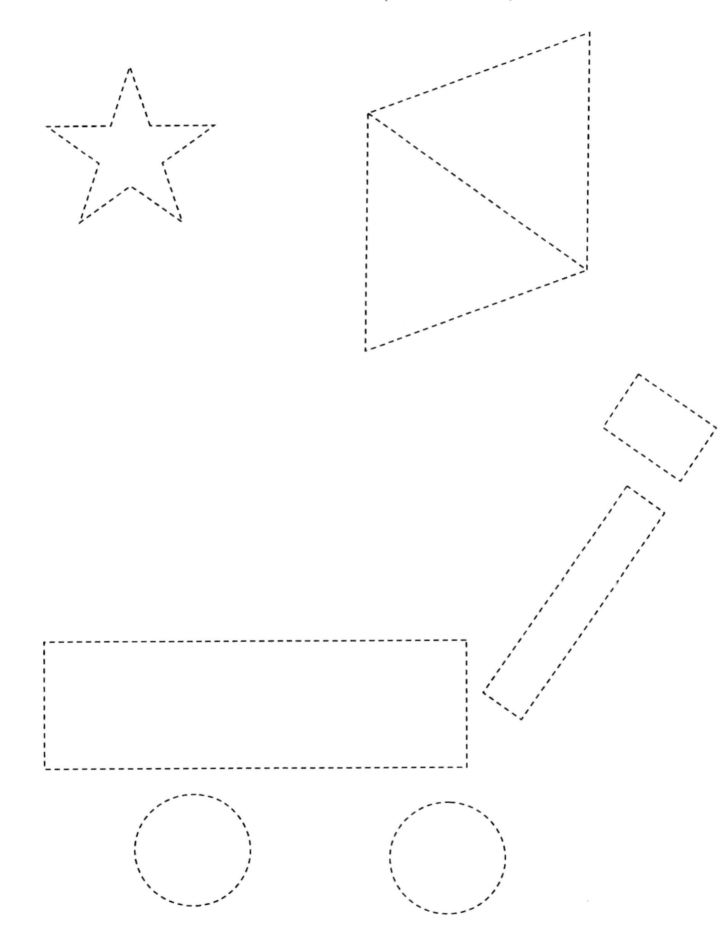

# STAR KITE AND WAGON

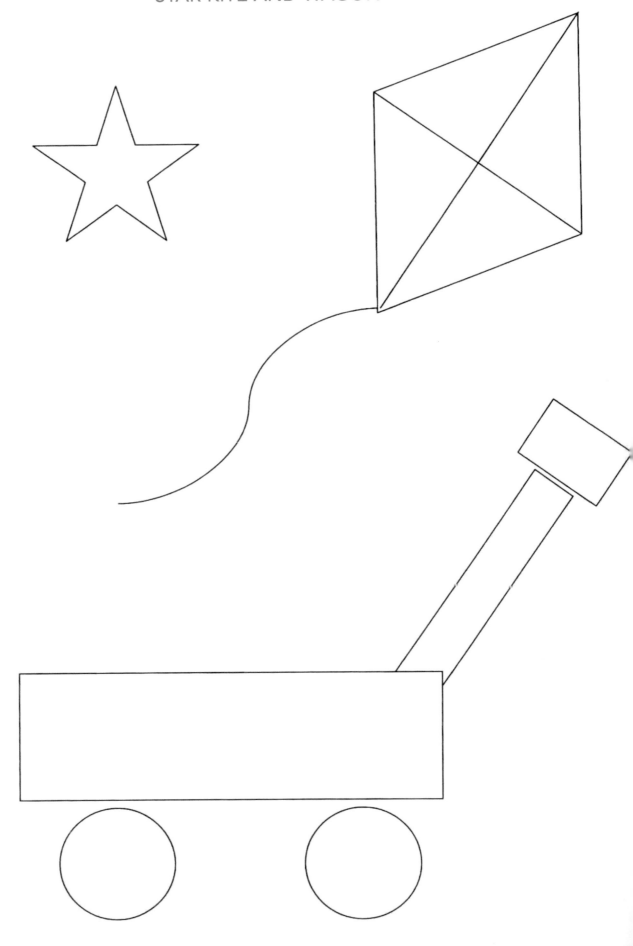

Printed in the United States
by Baker & Taylor Publisher Services